*the*

BIGGER WOMAN

# *the*

# BIGGER

# WOMAN

Armin Kabiri

Epigraph Publishing
Rhinebeck, New York

Paperback ISBN 978-1-948796-73-6

Book design by Colin Rolfe

Epigraph Books
22 East Market Street, Suite 304
Rhinebeck, New York 12572
(845) 876-4861
epigraphps.com

Man needs the bigger woman.

But she is only in MY imagination.

I am in love with the bigger woman.

The woman who appears through all
women and every breath of life.

The woman whose patterns sing
the melodies and drum the rhythms
of the earth.

Through her, I see every woman
who has crossed my path.

Through being in love with her, I love
all women.

Through loving women, I can find her.

She is the epitome of  heartbreak.

Her hand was stung by a wasp
in the middle of the night.

She woke in tears.

Out of her tears came
the greatest laughter.

Out of her laughter seeps
golden sap.

She accidentally hummed the most beautiful note.

How much this woman exists I cannot say.

For she can harden like a mirror or liquify into artful reflection.

When I cannot touch her,
 it upsets me.

But when I touch her, I want something more than touch.


I want everything.

Recently, I met a woman in
whom I saw the bigger woman.

However, she did not see
herself.

I left her weeping.


I saw her beyond time and space.

She was woven with the fabric of past,
present, and future.


I did not fall in love with her.
I fell in love with who she was
going to inevitably become.

Is the bigger woman myself?

If so, how only I AM.

I am the mountain which I climb.

Once I reach my peak, I dissolve
into my bigger self.

My bigger self then climbs my
even bigger self.

I have bitter feelings towards advice.
For how can anyone who does not
know who I am
advise me?

I would rather hear laughter
than misdirection.

If one should advise, let there
be greater emphasis on the
freedom of choice than the
advice itself.

But is this not advice?

I must not change under
the hand of the oppressor.


For the oppressor will change
under the hand of my truth.

The smaller woman must bare herself
before she can bare me.

Through the bigger woman I
can only give birth to the bigger child.

Does this make me a pregnant man?


If so, then birth I will give.

I will plant seeds in my own soil.

In a single grain, all sand can be seen.

But why do some grains give me
greater sight than others?

What do those fish of the abyss
think of those higher fish who
still feed from the sun?


For the fish of the abyss
have learned to become their own
sun.

Tiredness that consumes itself
becomes overawake.


I have landed upon dangerous
territory. I am in love with the
bigger woman inside of the
smaller woman.
Would it not be dishonest to profess
my love to the smaller woman?


Thus I weep.

If the bigger woman and eye
must be lonely, let us be lonely
together.

Could it be the bigger woman is the
earth?

How I see her outside of myself and
feel her within me.

Smaller men see me
like a distant planet.


They can only see the traces I
left lightyears ago.

Did the smaller woman show
me the bigger woman?


Or did the bigger woman speak
through the smaller woman?

THE BIGGER WOMAN

An empty cup is better than one
that is half full.


For the empty cup is full
in its emptiness.

How strange it is to be all sand
but love a single grain so much.


How strange it is that the grain
will never understand my love.


How strange my love is for the
grain that has shown me all sand.


And how in my seeing, I
became all sand.

More and more I feel like I am
the bigger woman.
How sad and free that makes me feel.
How only I am…

What makes man trade eternity
for a grain?

Is it not the bigger woman, who
as a grain, shows eternity?

The smaller woman lives with Maya.

Must I wait till she moves out?

On a cloudy day, the smaller
woman and eye decided to hike
to the peak of a waterfall.

Once we approached the peak, a
thunderous storm fell upon us.

We walked down the mountain
shivering in our nakedness.

When we approached
the bottom, the skies cleared and
the sun began to beam.


I realized I was standing next to the bigger
woman.

The breath of a moment
swept me to myself.

I learned that wisdom with
injured eyes cannot see
the bigger woman.

The bigger woman and the smaller
woman are like black and white keys
on a piano.

Together, they play chords.

In the silence, the black and white keys
are being laughed at
by the piano.

In my overawake loneliness, I
find the need to be lonely
with my guests.

And if I must have guests in my
loneliness, let the silence be
louder than words.

How could my guests and I
ever get to know each other
if we cannot be heartbroken
together?

Did I kill the smaller woman?

I only meant to whip her
but the seas willed my arrow.

When asking for change, let it
be like a warrior rather than a beggar.


However, if you must beg.
You must learn to beg for change
before you can beg for gold.

The smaller woman reveals
the bigger woman.

The bigger woman reveals all women.


The dance between them
reveals me to myself.

The smaller woman led me to
the bigger woman.

Now I'd like to make love to
myself.

The smaller woman could not look
me in the eyes.

Thus I could not bare her.


The bigger woman lives behind my eyes.

Last night, I told a guest I killed
the smaller woman.

She gasped.


Eye left laughing and weeping.

One who is willing to draw
must be willing to erase.


One who is willing to erase
must be willing to draw their
own blood.

One day, on the desert beach,
Africa revealed herself to me.


I could not tell if she was showing me
days of most distant past
or most distant future.

How does the bigger man
inspire the bigger woman
without changing her?

For she must change herself.




I treat the bigger woman like a
boomerang.

If she does not come back, she is either
injured or I did not throw her
hard enough.

In the intoxicated night, I met the
bigger woman.

Many months later, I arrived
at her house with a serpent.

This time I was much bigger than her.

On the last night she got bit.

A bigger leap she was about to take.

Hopefully one day we will meet
again in deeper seas and higher skies.

One must learn to proceed
without caution.


However, one must be not so cautious
of caution itself.

Only the woman who could
bare me in the darkest night,

could see me
through the blinding light.

It is through the silences
of the smaller woman
that I have learned to hear
the echoes of her bigger self.

I met a grain of sand who made me
believe I could make such a connection
with any grain.

After meeting smaller grains
I became heartbroken.

However, as I stepped into the jungle,
I looked at the desert from afar
and she laughed at me.

Is the bigger woman part
of the bigger man?


Or are they both a part of who
eye am?